# VERNAL POOL

# VERNAL POOL

## David Shaddock

ISBN- 13:978-0692316832

*Kelsay Books*
White Violet Press
www.kelsaybooks.com

*For Anita Barrows and Dawn McGuire*

# Acknowledgements

Thanks to Station House Journal for the publication of a selection of these sonnets.

Thanks to Anita Barrows, Dawn McGuire, Chana Bloch, Steve Kowit, Fred Marchant, Rabbis Burt Jacobson, Diane Elliot and the members of the Colrain Manuscript Conference for advice and support

Thanks to John Oliver Simon for showing me the possibilities of this hendecasyllabic, 4 4 3 3 form.

The Unknown Known refers to a film of that name by Errol Morris

The last 18 poems are inspired by translations of the Psalms by Rabbi Zalman Schacter Shalomi in *Psalms in a Translation for Praying,* published in 2014 by Aleph.

# Contents

## II.EIGHTEEN PSALMS

# I.

# THE JILTED BRIDE MOON

# Arrival

You arrive to the light hissing of airlocks

The screech of brakes metal on metal. You float

Down on the wind like a eucalyptus leaf.

The dog barks as you pull into the driveway.


The numbers line up, the tumblers click in place

The children start to play in the living room.

The accordion streetcar doors slide open

The dome light comes on when you shut off the key.


Just two more oar pulls and the silent tender

Arrives at the dock, the fire truck's red lights splash

On the pleated paper blinds, elevator


Doors open to labor and delivery.

The first drops of rain hit the skylight, you wake

And check your cell phone. One text from the airport.

Vernal Pool

They were playing the hits from '66 on
KFOG this morning.  I was meeting my wife
At the oncologist.  Don't be alarmed it's
All good, they can go cell by cell to get clean


Margins these days.  She doesn't even need much
Radiation.  I was expecting something
Like Iron Butterfly, but it was all Otis
The Byrds, Dylan.  To celebrate we walked north

From Inspiration Point.  Despite the long drought
There were orange poppies and forget-me-nots
Vernal pools with a chorus of croaking frogs.

I thought of Cape Ann, years ago, how we listened
For hours to the bullfrogs and spring peepers
Convinced that we'd found the ur source of music.

## Near Vacaville

The late spring rains on the nitrogen rich cow
Pasture make the grass a psychedelic green
You're sure you've seen before, but that can't be true
Since you've just arrived here from some exotic

Planet, catching up with the local habits.
You have a backstory with these humans, this
You get.  It's your wife in that dress, your dog who's
Snoring along in the back seat.  So all right

Let's go to Sacramento!  Are we all late
For a play?  Do we all have grandchildren with
A big part in "Cats" by Andrew Lloyd Weber?

I think we can do this, fellow humans, while
The aching green still echoes in our mind's eye
And hunger rumbles in our tummy's fun place.

# New Car

Shards of Gold Rush era villages poke through

The cracked dry clay of the drought-shrunk reservoir.

Prisoners who blew .08 or shrugged off

Probation pick up the baggies and windblown


Candy wrappers from the weed-choked white guardrails.

We're out for a test run in our new hybrid

So quiet the satellite radio smooth jazz

Feels like it's inside us, bass backbone, snare toes.


The highlighted figure on the dashboard tells how

We rock between gas and electric.  I hope

The future mentions we were good, that we tried.


Remember that cafe right on the Yuba

Where we'd stop after camping at Blue Lakes?

Is it still there?  Does that same couple own it?

# Midsummer

The carpenter bees are killing the peach tree.
The pear tomatoes go from near perfect to
Overripe overnight.  Bush lupine and red
Paintbrush in the high country, corn lilies done

Yellow leaves drooping.  The all-star break can't come
Too soon for the Giants.  I like the smell of
Melting ice in the parking lot from the fish
Store.  I even like the half an hour flagman

Wait coming back from the weekend.  Radio
Crackles, then a pair of asphalt filled dump trucks
And the sign turns from red to yellow.  Descent

Beckons, wrote Williams, as the ascent beckoned.
No harm in asking for a fifteenth line, though
You already know what the answer will be.

# Flung

We're flung here, stuck to the wall, an errant toss
Of pizza dough, an overly violent
Pool break, the mud behind a spinning car wheel
A splotch of something that's best left unmentioned

But we read the entrails of special chickens
Send neutrons at each other through tubes under
Mountains, model nanoseconds after the
Big Bang, wonder what the Hanged Man upside down

Means.  The boys on one side girls on the other
Waiting to see who we get paired with for the
Mexican Hat Dance.  How astonishing to

Find it's you, my love, your knee curled at my back
One point on a vast grid of time and space, one
Digit in a line of numbers, a warmth there.

# Walk

I walk along Alhambra past the Safeway
And CVS, on past the strip mall card club
And the asphalt junior high that looks to me
Like a repurposed army base.  Everywhere God

The Bal Shem taught, sunlight on the parking lot
The fat geese by the fountain, the ivy walled
Branch library, every word in every book
The bound Delta hydrology reports, Leaves

Of Grass the deathbed edition, bound Sunsets
From the fifties in their yearly cardboard sleeves.
A cool drink from the old porcelain fountain

And I'm on my way, out past the park, broad leaf
Maple, trikes on lawn, new waxed Silverado
Billowing curtains, someone's music playing.

## Shabbes Eve

The moon is rummaging around the garden
Splintering the bean poles, knocking the old gate
Off its hinges, drinking the beer I left out
For the slugs.  It's the flat of tomato starts

She's after, so I threw a sheet over them
At bedtime.  They say the blood orange moon will
Drink the piss out of your body, but don't think

The jilted bride moon is much better, snagging
her veil on the bougainvillea then flailing
At the window, jittering the points that hold

The panes in place.  Don't be angry, Shekinah.
I'm a wayward husband, drunk half the week, but
I left you some challah out on the table.

# Station

A train sighs toward Anytown USA
Station.  Trash everywhere, concertina wire
Chunks of scrap rebar, smashed concrete like a hoard
Of medieval weaponry.  Everything's broken

It says in Kabbalah, because creation
Couldn't hold the sparks of God's light and shattered
Into a million fragments.  Lots with leaky
Drums, clotheslines behind a few makeshift houses.

You detrain amidst a swirl of skirts and suits
Past the candy stand and florist, up the long
Escalator out to the pumping city.

All day you pretend you're fine, but the broken
Plinths and half buried tires in the estuary
Need you, since you were a boy you have known that.

# Shim

I keep trying to slip a shim in between
Names and objects.  Poetry, like silicone
Caulk from a pressurized nozzle, filling voids
It helps to create.  Those are my gills the inch

Long Coho fry at Lagunitas Creek are
Finning.  I know because only drowning men
Could see him, because even four-toed sloth me
Could learn to dance all night at the Avalon

Because I read The Ohlone Way on acid
At Blake Street, because I heard Northrup Frye talk
About Yeats' A Vision at I-House the day

Reagan's helicopters teargassed Sproul Plaza
Because my animal pillow friends told me
And then later I read Heinlein by flashlight.

# My Poems

I want my poems to do better than me.
It is the most natural thing in the world.
I want to help them over the wall I crashed
Give them the stylish clothes my parents couldn't.

Must my poems listen to the Dead all the way
From Albuquerque to LA on acid
Rouse up my mother then crash for three days, wake
And drink three cans of frozen OJ, peeling

The cardboardy stuff and plunking the frozen
Core into a blue pitcher of hot water?
Must they reread all my high school Alan Watts books?

Do I tell them when they believe from YouTube
That the FDA secretly makes cancer
That's crazy, the world's not lined up against you?

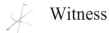

# Witness

I've decided to be a witness though I
Haven't been subpoenaed.  I want to tell them
What I saw downtown, out on the dark highway
In the village square.  I want to help both sides

To prosecute, to damn and condemn, to send
The miscreants straight to the hell they richly
deserve, but I also want to exonerate
The innocent, frame things in the right context

Convince the jury that the truth is complex
That it weaves through a narrative like a vein
Of serpentine.  They say I'm likely guilty

Myself, that I'm hiding what happened outside
In the car, in the backroom, on the vast plain
When my mind was on vacation and my hands

## BART Station

How tired you get pushing against gravity
Making sure the earth doesn't fall into space
Forever, spinning the day, keeping steady
Time while breathing back and forth with the forest.

It starts with synching up your own heartbeat and
The Greenwich, England Cesium clock, minding
As well the precession of the equinoxes
With a weather eye out for asteroids or

Solar flares.  You had inklings, but you found
Out it was up to you and only you on
March 9th, 2002, coming up the long

Escalator from Montgomery Street BART
The sun breaking through scudding clouds, the two string
Violin, the old man's eyes, the red streetcar.

# The Unknown Known

Rumsfeld, but the line was too long so we just
Had pizza and talked about frames and the slow
Denouement between "fin" and popcorn lobby.
The women who see everything, the Sikh taxis

Pulling up and leaving.  I said Whitman, you
Didn't argue, his Lincoln those quick glimpses
Of the morning ride from the Summer White House
Which Bush obviously debased but possible

Now at all?  They're ex-New Yorkers you can tell
By the gloves, and the talk turned to Duncan and
Denise, is it art's job just to imagine

Evil, or as Denise maintained, to condemn
It?  The reviews spoke of an elegiac tone
But it's too late and we don't feel like waiting.

# Corrida

The corrida about the cartel king's middle
Finger showing up in El Presidente's
French fries went viral, Sinaloa downloads
Alone enough to crash the system.  Chinga

Tu madre authority being a well
Loved sentiment from Michoacan dirt farms
To the gringo groveling Zocalo tour
Touts who would like to tell them where to shove it

When the ballad of El Chapo's finger soars
From the trashcan fire encampment radios.
The balding ex Baghdad buddy DEA

Guys download it too, in their Holiday Inn
Hotel room in Acapulco.  Viva drug punks
Viva the meth snorting Iowa farmboys.

# Nativity Scene

O little corporation alone in the
Manger, who will keep the nipping wolves at bay?
You can hear, at night, the unions howl, the taxmen
Circling in the woods, the whooshing raptor wings

Of the regulators flying low above
The treetops. O virgin born corporation
Child not of man but of God, who will stand guard
Over you in the wilderness? I will says

Black-robed Alito. I will says wise Roberts
Silent Thomas out of Africa. O lamb
Of God let us nurse you, protect your precious

Bleats as speech. You will found vast kingdoms
Own buildings tall as mountains, but never will
We leave your side, or let the rabble at you.

# Catfish

You don't get to be a 120
Pound channel catfish by snapping at any
Damn lure they throw at you, plastic night crawlers
Or wounded crawdads.  You learn by experience

To soft mouth the bait, spit out the hook, look out
For the props of ski boats or the intake pipes
Of siphons.  Let the sturgeon eat all your roe
The salt water incursion drive you half way

Up to Stockton.  High flows, no snow, it's the same
To you, a self, inviolate, finning the mud
Scanning for freshwater clams with your whiskers.

Consider, as telomeres fray, cataracts
Cloud our vision and plaques clog our arteries
Why species like catfish spurned evolution.

# Hospital

The white hospital looked just like Ikea
Everything clean and organized the liver
Doctors on the second floor, beige leather couches
For cancer, a row of amazing vending

Machines down a long corridor, they light up
And play a typical folk song that will go
With the food, shakuhachi for your sushi
A weird Bulgarian chorus for Kavarma.

The surgery unit is appealing, those clamps
And retractors might work in our kitchen.
A number of the nurses seemed to be twins.

The patients enjoyed the confusion.  The men
With breast buds were popular.  God was in
Swedenborg Chapel, I wanted to stay there.

# Something

It's all such fal dara, history, the rise
Of this and that, the fall of some such, meaning
Leaking away like a faulty sump, who cares
For the vendors, the Tijuana Chiclet kids

Or for that matter the guys who shoe the race
Horses or ride a hunch, ignoring the tide
Of derision.  Our hopes for super symmetry
Abandoned, left out in the rain like piles

Of newspaper.  Hawks and hawkers, labor cries
A trail of entrails, charmed quarks, the flight of the
Valkyries, all the tea in China, the great

And terrible Khan, mangled tribals. A kiss
Across your dry lips, your sly and furtive tongue
How I long for that, something to hold onto.

# Tradeoff

All my near-misses have backstories. Those black
Ice three sixties in the Econoline were
At dawn in trafficless Wyoming because
I told the truck stop cashier that's too much change.

There's always tradeoffs. Finish your lasagna
If you want some leftover birthday cake. I
won't drop acid till the last hour of my shift
at the warehouse. If the A's win the pennant,

I'll wear green socks for a year. You can't go Hi
it's me, God, David, remember the time I
blah de blahed? It's more like the carbon exchange

Where you plant some trees to offset your smokestacks.
They keep track at the Capital. That's why I'm
Still here, I flossed and took the dog out to pee.

# Exhibit

I expected more about me in your art
Exhibit.  Everything was from before we met
Displayed like pre-Columbian artifacts.
I could hear your rejoinder that it was my

Dream, so I didn't complain.  But the hubcaps
From your old Beatle and so forth, and then not
Even the jacket from the Otis album
You played on our first date. This was not as Jung

Would say a big dream.  But what if happiness
Is like that, recontextualized at a
Drop of the hat.  Or if the you here is me?

I didn't mention it when you called from Portland
Talking about the good times with your sister.
But this part of me not beamed on, what is it?

# Dead Poets

Even the dead are looking for publishers.
Norton is apparently ignoring its
Backlist, they want out of their once lucrative
Contracts, they're sure there's a posthumous book or

Two just waiting for a sensitive scholar.
They care at New Directions, Copper Canyon
I tell them has a promising new intern
Who loves your work.  The Internet creates new

Readers all the time.  I was nice to Denise
So they all want my ear. Three a.m.'s my me
Time, but now I'm hit with a clamor on my way

To the bathroom.  I'm polite to everyone
But my own work is beginning to suffer.
I keep a baseball bat ready, just in case.

## Cornell Box

These sonnets are a bit like Cornell boxes.
Everything inside becomes its own little world.
Canaries and apothecary bottles filled with
Colored marbles--but who knows why no one picked

Up the kennel, or why the guy by the Fox
Thought I was strapped.  My sister put the gold bands
From Daddy's Panatelas on her finger
And rehearsed her wedding day in the living

Room.  I heard him tell the guards I was packing
But they barely patted me down.  In his prime
He spun a wheel to pick the songs.  Finally

The dog's owner came rushing to the baggage.
She'd been lost.  I love the jagged scraps of French
Wallpaper, all the stars like gaping bird mouths.

## Mood Swing

Who if I cried out and so forth, but today
I don't feel existentially lonely
Though it remains just a microns-thin membrane
Away.  I am so pleased that at 8:03

Beauty is nothing but the start of beauty
That I want to call home, though who knows who that
Would mean dialing.  Help me Jesus I'm on
My knees just drove by waving.  Every angel

Terrible or not is wasting his time on
Bipolar me, I'm beyond help at both ends
Of my mood swings.  This is not my morning toke

Or the cappuccino talking.  The chairs here
Have low back support.  Last night, without a word
We decided not to stay for the ending.

# Live Oak Park

This beautiful streamside through overhung redwoods
Is populated by the affectively
Disregulated and those who fail to choose
Our consensual realities. They offer

My dog half of their breakfast, sensing something
Familiar in her animal needs. They
Lack the learned discernment of the propertied.
Half a McDonald's egg sandwich her reward

For impudence, but they wave off I'm sorry.
The poor share, the rich steal, so it has always
Been, though God groans on high. He gave this idyll

To fill with toothless laughter, water strider
In the still pool, an empty pack of Camel
Filters, a sea-green bottle of Mountain Dew.

# Shower

I don't want to go all Robinson Jeffers
But standing in line for a propane heated
Shower at the Tuolumne Meadows campground
With a bunch of smelly backpackers makes me

Wonder what the hell we're doing here, farting
And fracking and fucking up the planet. True
The worst thing here is my up yours attitude
Entitled and suspicious though light bathed for

Days, scrambling up granite while little pikas
Dart between rock piles and striated clouds turn
The dappled gray glacier smoothed surfaces

Into billowing pillows soft on the eyes
Like a mother. Enough you'd think to quash
The mind gash that keeps me an other, but no.

# Quick

Quick like a pronghorn antelope in Jackson
Quicker than lightning in the rear view mirror
Quick like shame, quick like knowing and unknowing
In the same instant. Quick as glint of a knife

In the parking lot. Quick as falling in love
Or dying. Quick as a tongue of bright flame
From the last coals in the campfire flashing shapes
And color. Quick as karma, quick as ardor.

Quick as the transmigration of souls, of flocks
Of redwing blackbirds from the stubbly rice field.
Quick as knowing God's mind, seeing everything

Rise up like droplets in a fountain fly free
Of the pattern, become the pattern, become
Shadows on the pebble path, the garden wall.

# Satellite Photo

Until they got satellite pictures from space
No one knew how round and beautiful I was.
My left and right were always fighting.  Stop it
I'd say, we're all one, but they wouldn't listen.

My lungs were jealous of my kidneys, my heart
Would not be seen out in public with my mind
And all feared the jungle dwelling genitals
Who were only pretending to be Christian.

Ragtag armies ruled my thoughtstream, promising
The world, creating hope, then falling into
Petty fights over food or philosophy.

Look I'd say when the first verdant striated
Images came out, here is truth: we are all
One organ.  All the voices chimed, then silence.

# II

# EIGHTEEN PSALMS

1.

You finish my sentences like we're a long
Married couple, discern my state, track my tacks
Between fantasy and despair, mark the start
Of my day and its ending. You speak through me

When I praise, when I doubt. Your voice in my head
Is like a whiff of jazz from a passing car
Its few notes a cradle. Ecstasy a door
To you; you are there in the Hells I create

For myself with guilt and recrimination.
I find you in my dreams when I am walking
Down an endless corridor, or the second

I wake like a newborn, trying to blink out
The light. The old song says hate those who deny
You, but that's not true, cruelty just makes me sad.

*After Psalm 139*

2.


Infants babble a song of praise to you, Yah

You take strength from the first word a toddler speaks.

The breaching juvenile humpback sings your praise

Cormorants swirling an anchovy boil chime in.


I start each day by asking who but you, Yah

Cast the firmament upon the waters, who

Watered the firmament with rivers and lakes?  Who

Put life in my step, who made sure I was not blind


When I woke?  Somewhere within the reach of my

Mind is a knowledge almost as vast as yours

A dazzling fireworks show with no finale


Galaxies frizzling down from the canisters.

Praise the range of our nature: angel or poised

To strike, and praise the Noh stage on which it plays.

*After Psalm 8*

3.


Like a mother, Yah, you are both vividly

Inside me and gone forever. I am both

Bereft and exalted. My mouth makes the O

Of having nothing to suckle. But always


A next breath, a conviction, out of nowhere

That you are just ahead, around the corner

Down the path to the old house. Why elude me

Yah, why must I toggle from intimation


To despair? Shame like a hatching worm breaks out

In the middle of prayer, at the moment

The poem begins to ebb. Is it my mind


Or are they out there, laughing and sharpening

Their knives? Let them. At last the praise urge returns

And I wake up like Jacob, bruised and new-named.

*After Psalm 22*

4.


Cut school and took my mom's white Valiant up

One to Big Sur. Looking down at floating gulls

Whitecapped boulders, kelp surging, the slo-mo spray

Display, I had, and still have, no adequate


Response to your splendor, Yah. Your word speaks sun

Into the day, rainbows the wave crashed foam, prisms

Drop flecked glasses with a hundred iterations

Of your glory. How do I live, after that?


A question that daily vexes. Am I high

On my ego, am I low because I can't

Accept the boundless love you pour into this


World? Half awake, I mumble prayers to you

Write poems that approximate gratitude.

May they all be acceptable in your sight.

*After Psalm 19*

5.


Is that your hand under the small of my back,
Guiding levitation?  My wife is asleep
So it must be you, Yah lifting me up from
The violent roil of my dreams.  So many

Bastards, inside and out, stealing the grandkids
Fucking my wife.  But here it is light again
Yah, hardly a bird even singing, and I
Am rising into your silence.  Just being

Alive is my morning prayer.  Comfort me
Dear one.  Still my jaw that has been grinding all
Night, rechewing slights, stifling my cry for help

So I do not let them find my position.
You know what we're like here, but you still remain
Pleased when I write to you, or call out your name.

*After Psalm 5*

6.


I'm walking and toggling all day between fear

And joy. If joy is my true home, whose hand pulls

The thread that starts the unravel? I'm thinking

It's me who can't get it right, but maybe that's


The way it is for you as well, a harvest

Sukkah one minute, an angry flood the next.

Praise and lament, love and anger, is it all

Music to your ear, Yah, a clubfooted stomping


As sweet to you as a timbrel laced toe dance?

Don't hide both your faces from me, and I won't

Hide both of mine. I can't shake despair today.


It's pulsing though me with every heartbeat.

Make me a home in your sadness, invite us

To your tent to recall what we almost were.

*After Psalm 27*

7.


More years behind than ahead, Yah.  I look at
My hands, think how strange to remember the things
They held as a child.  Dovbear Spivak, my great
Uncle, with a Russian fur hat, had huge hands.


Cossacks, pogroms.  What's he talking about?  Bad
Things happened to the Jews a long time ago.
Later I read about Audie Murphy taking
Out a German machine gun nest by himself.


Pound, Eliot, all anti-Semites, leftist
Rally speakers shouting about the Jewish
Media.  Always dread, but love inside me


As well.  The words come, I learn more every day.
They're from you, Yah.  You fill up these fourteen
Lines like wine in a cup.  I drink first, then pass.

*After Psalm 3*

8.

*for Robin Williams*

A mob in my mind—torches, acrimony.

I wake in a sweat, a pool of salt water

On my pillow.  I can't move, my bones feel like

Paste, my muscles a mess of shredded paper.


God holds you over the burning fire like a

Loathesome spider I read in Perry Miller's

Books on the Puritans, then dropped LSD

And went to the Avalon.  At the time that


Seemed like an answer, but certainties erode.

You're indicted from the moment you are born

Your pretention exposed, the worm in your heart


Gone viral on YouTube.  You're right, Yah.  I need

Your mercy more than I could have imagined.

Comfort me, kick the bastards out of my head!

*After Psalm 6*

50

9.


Yah how they blaspheme.  They say kill and your name
In the same sentence, stir up mobs, show no shame
Over carnage.  Leaders plot and calculate, count
Votes instead of bodies while the numbers mount.

Where shall I turn for comfort?  I want to go
Home, to your land, where springs run clear, but I know
It exists only in my longing.  Anger
Strangles me, my inaction is no better

Than the rabble roil.  "I've seeded the world
With Tzadikim, planted the truth in your brain.
Life and death here before you, sane and insane.

Stop raging if you want a God without rage.
Imagine peace and it comes into being.
You're my Moses, I am the slave you're freeing. "

*After Psalm 2*

# 10.

It was sad to buck out the old freestone peach
Tree, though in truth for years the fruit was mealy.
The saw whirl stilled my thoughts a moment, that was
A blessing in itself.  So many useless

Thoughts, like somebody left a radio on
In the trashcan.  Help me, Yah! I don 't want to
Be lonely, saying to a bunch of strangers
In the lunch room, after all my kids have their

Own lives to lead.  But there is a counterforce
To death, I've sensed it.  A leather-bound letterpress book
Of poems like my friend Anita gave me--

A shudder of pleasure.  The old forms still hold
Yah, the daily Seder.  Better poets half
My age, but do they know the spring you showed me?

*After Psalm 4*

11.


"Hands up don't shoot" the protestors march but cops

Don't stop. I tried being Buddhist—they're afraid

Just like me--but the kid was going down when

They shot off the top of his head. *They devour*


*My people as casually as they chow down*

*A sandwich... They turn on the poor as if they*

*Were the enemy.* Same shit, different age.

I'm so done with non-attachment. There's nothing


Good to say about these racist bullies or

The thugs they work for. Tzaddik Zalman, Denise--

Grafts of you in my mind. A wan melody


From a reed flute in a storm. My eyes wind-teared.

It's a prayer, plaintive like shakuhachi

But angry: Yah stop this endless killing.

*After Psalm 14*

12.


Everything's postmodern, Yah, I can barely
Stand it anymore.  I learned how to write from
Pound, *news that stays news*, then later learned how
Sickening was the stretch of his hatred.  No one

Would dare take up his cudgel after that, all's
Hedged with indeterminacy.  Help
My hand toward truth, Yah, you be my reader
See how straight a line I draw from my heart to

The page.  Half the good people are all Dawkins
And seeing what is done in your name who can blame
Them?  In truth the rewards I seek from you far

Outstrip the weakness of my faith.  Only when
I'm most desperate do I not hold back my
Prayer, and only when no one else is there.

*After Psalm 17*

13.


My four month grandson lights up when he sees me
With a smile that is rounder on one side.
It's the you in me he sees, Yah, not the me
Who twizzles on the frayed ends of my desires

Who scours the archives and keeps endless tallies
Of my detractors, the Costco high piled cart
Me who runs his wine fueled mouth on politics
Or loses his Corolla keys and then flirts

With the Avis lady.  The six directions
All sage smudged clean by an infant's innocence.
Your hierophant, Yah, guiding my steps up to

Your throne, loves progress, one then many torment
Free seconds, the clear plastic kitchen chairs where
We sit, his little fists rooting, those blue eyes.

*After Psalm 16*

14.


I hate it when you look at me like that, Yah.

Yet I always go back to the mirror for

More.  What do you see?  A thin filament glow

In the cloudy eye globe.  Maybe just enough


For a night light.  Please don't let it go out, it's

On a timer.  I keep talking to myself

And calling it prayer.  I'm watching my thoughts

Grow ever more suspicious—who took my cellphone


Who's my wife talking to?  I listen to my

Son blame everyone but himself for trouble—

Did he learn that from me?  Sometimes the words come


From you, most of the time they are only mine.

Cut the bullshit, be tough, be kind to myself.

I can't get it right, Yah.  That's why I need you.

*After Psalm 26*

15.


The fullness of fractals falling from fountains

Kaleidoscopic twists make new galaxies

Spirals, ellipses pinging Hubble's tuning

Fork--spherical music download to your head


Agate Beach Oregon 1968 fire

Sparking driftwood Sufi twisting exploding

Consciousness.  Who is free enough of mother

To receive this, who has begged her forgiveness?


Chris and Jeff and I, seawater beading our

Naked bodies?  Fifty years.  Nothing to you

Yah, who hums every atom into its own


Resonant existence.  How long before your

Gate?  Pry open my grip, pour me like water

Fire hose blast or a fog congealing mist.

*After Psalm 24*

16.

*An Aleph Bet song of David*

Ashamed to be ashamed here before you, Yah.

Better to put that all aside, remember

Childhood, when faith came unbidden, no hint of

Disgrace looming over my soul.  This morning,


Early on, I rose to pray in gratitude

For all your blessings, for the fullness of this

Green Earth, for your spirit which flows down here from

Heaven.  Though I blew off my lonely mother


Ignoring her plight as a still young widow

Just now you stopped my guilt spiral with your great

Kindness.  Teach me to treat myself better, Yah


Let your great love light my path through this gray world.

May your mercy redound through merciful acts

Now in this silent moment, broken open.

*After Psalm 25*

58

17.

*An Aleph Bet song of David (cont.)*

Only by grace do I fall asleep at night.  You
Pour your love over me, Yah in these hours so
Quiet I can almost hear it flowing.  You
Repair the torn fringe, whisper in my sleep the

Secrets you save for the awakened ones, the
Tzadikim who live the inner Torah, who
Understand the worlds within words, but who have
Volunteered to stay and be spark gatherers

World healers.  In the vast unconscious I'm an
X, a placeholder, but you see more in me
Yah then I see, you forgive my shortcomings

Zero out my sins, find where I left my car
Allow me somehow to catch the last flight
Before I wake and reenter my body.

*After Psalm 25*

18.

Even on a sunny day death's shadow looms.
A car careens, a mugger lurks, something turns
Up on a routine lab test.  Yet here I am
Across the street, ready to lead my old dog

For a run in the park, ready for a cool
Drink from the fountain.  Why not believe it's your
Strength I lean on, that fear of your rebuke stays
My greed and malice?  Even the dark valleys

I create for myself so far have always
Brightened, and the sharp pains of my losses have dulled
Just as your consoling voice in my mind's ear

Promised.  Will my kids have jobs or stay off drugs?
Will my love and I have a few more unvexed
Years?  It's your voice I hear saying yes, we will.

*After Psalm 23*

# Notes

p. 20. Shekinah: In Jewish mysticism, the female emanation of God, also identified as the Sabbath Bride.

p. 44 ff. Yah: "A breath/spirit-like name for God that is associated with the attribute of compassion." Rabbi Zalman Schacter-Shalomi, *Psalms in a translation for praying,* p. iv.

p. 51. Tzadikim: Righteous, holy individuals.

p. 53. Hands up don't shoot: Refers to a protest slogan following the police shooting of an unarmed man in Ferguson, Missouri, August 14, 2014.

# About the Author

David Shaddock's poems have won the Ruah Magazine Power of Poetry Award for a collection of spiritual poems, and the International Peace Poem Prize, among other honors. His poems have appeared in such journals as Tikkun and Mother Jones. His books include *In This Place Where* Something's Missing *Lives* with an afterword by Rabbi Arthur Waskow, and *Dreams Are Another Set of Muscles,* with an introduction by Denise Levertov. His play, "In A Company of Seekers," was performed at the 2012 Festival of Two Worlds in Spoleto, Italy. He holds a PhD in psychoanalytic research from Middlesex University London and is the author of two nonfiction books on relationships and couples therapy. He maintains a private psychotherapy practice in Oakland and lives with his family in Berkeley.

Poem prayers
Send Vienella
+ Defense
Michael glaser
Nativity scene
unknown known

witness
walk
vomit pool
ur language